Skipping Stones

Skipping Stones

RYAN DIAZ

RESOURCE *Publications* · Eugene, Oregon

SKIPPING STONES

Resource Publications
An Imprint of Wipf and Stock Publishers
199 W. 8th Ave., Suite 3
Eugene, OR 97401

www.wipfandstock.com

PAPERBACK ISBN: 978-1-6667-3864-3
HARDCOVER ISBN: 978-1-6667-9962-0
EBOOK ISBN: 978-1-6667-9963-7

MAY 25, 2022 5:14 AM

To the memory
of
Nerida Rivera

I dislike the idea of being a religious poet.
I would prefer to be a poet for whom religious things matter intensley.

—ROWAN WILLIAMS

CONTENTS

ACKNOWLEDGEMENTS

Ekstasis

The Dewdrop

Writeresque

In Parentheses

PLATITUDES

I got a call from a friend
That his brother of twenty-four
Had died, a heart attack.
I had no words of comfort,
So I mumbled something
About prayer, platitudes
Designed to fill the awkward
Silence. But what else can you say
In the face of unnatural
Loss. Isn't that the point of prayer?
To say what can't be said out loud
In hopes that God might hear it too—
The wordless groans of faithless hearts
Looking to make sense of it all
And why twenty-four-year-olds die
Before their appointed time.

ON MY INABILITY TO PRAY

I sit with my back to a tree, my face
Facing a little inlet sparkling
With stolen treasure. The sun's light a victim
Of the crystalline waters below,
Trapped now like jewels in a dragon's hoard,
Flickering back and forth across the tide,
Perpetually searching for a way back
Home. And like that light, my prayers are locked
In a heart-shaped box cut off from my lips,
Endlessly searching for a way
To escape. A place where they'd be heard.
Free to be answered or unanswered,
Free to roam the halls of divine providence,
Free to be what they were made to be—
Brilliant beams of latent potential,
Pockets of faith ready to burst, filling
Creation with the incense of belief.

But for now, they're trapped in this heart-shaped box.
Solar jewels sinking beneath the water's edge
Longing to light the depths of the deep.

SKIPPING STONES

Little pebbles bounce along the old Bone Pond,
Skimming along the glass like rainwater,
Leaving concentric circles in their wake,
Straining with all their might to meet the edge,
Hopelessly weighed down by the illusion
Of buoyancy. Each time a stone is cast
We cross our fingers and close our eyes.
Hoping, praying that our little stone won't sink,
Little boys playing at God, defying
Gravity and Newton and all the things
That would make a good stone sink. Hoping, Praying
That our arms are strong and our aim is true
And that our little stones would do what we couldn't do—
Make it to the other side without drowning,
Without being pulled under, swallowed whole,
With nothing but fading circles to
Remember them by—little pebbles
sinking, longing for the water's edge,
Cast like prayers in the dead of night,
Hoping to find a listening ear.

MAUNDY THURSDAY

All at once, I am traitor and friend,
Judas in the still night pursing his lips
Preparing to land a blow both sharp and sweet,
Gilded with silver, more brand than a kiss.

And yet, each time he welcomes me home
And beckons me to uncover my feet,
Not to expose, but to attend my sores
And with gentle hands offer sweet relief.

Somedays, I fail and betray him with lips
On others, I pledge to fight to the end.
No matter the day he responds the same.
He calls me by name and pronounces me friend.

Each day, I'm in the garden again,
Silent, spellbound, unsure what to say.
He stands before me and I must decide,
Who will I be on this Maundy Thursday?

THEOTOKOS

You are holy ground, the maiden mother,
A thin place where the transcendent meets flesh,
A tabernacle of body and breath.

We are holy ground, jars of broken clay,
Dry souls quenched by Pentecostal rain,
Imbued with the dew of new creation.

You are holy ground, you reading this now,
You are a reliquary of grace,
Deceptively mundane, brimming with wonder,
A space fit to bear the presence of God.

WHAT ARE SHADOWS?

What are shadows but abstractions of light,
Vague impressions of greater glory,
Alive only briefly, short passing things,

Owing their existence to another;
Shrinking as soon as the sun dips below
The outer edge of the horizon.

And one day, all the shadows will cease to be
For the darkness will have no place to hide
And evil will be no thing. Feeing,

Like a shadow shrinking before the sun.

KINTSUGI

Where do good things go when they cease to be well,
When they lose the luster of innocence,
Becoming all that is unbecoming?

And who restores all the broken things?
Who fills the artist's cracks with gold,
Banishing the blemishes left behind?

Who mends the shattered things, making them whole,
Returning goodness to good things gone bad,
Restoring what was lost in the breaking?

Give me sight to see beauty in broken things,
Turn these wounded palms into mending hands,
Send me to to the place the good things go,

Where good things cease to be well.

VANITY

Green fingers stretch out against azure skies,
A cool breeze slipping between the digits
As they try in vain to catch the west wind.

Below, a river fights against its flow,
Raging against its predestined course
Only to give up and cede to the sea.

And we all strain against gravity's weight,
Perpetually gazing at the sun,
Longing to loosen these fetters and fly.

A LESSON IN PRAYER

Breathe, savor each breath,
Summon the courage to
Take another breath.

Now is not the time for words,
Just breathe, savor each breath,
Let your heart do the talking.

Follow the rhythms,
Breathe in time to the beat,
Savor the silent words,

Linger over the things
You left unsaid. Then breathe,
Now is not the time for words.

Instead, follow the silence
And breathe, savor each breath,
Wait for the words born in quiet

And then be quiet.
Now is not the time for words.
Just breathe, savor each breath.

PASSING THE PEACE

How does one pass the peace? Is it as simple
As pressing fingers and thumbs into the
Cleft of your palms, leaving the remaining
Digits to dance in their place while you chant
Peace be with you in a monotone drawl.

Who's to say if peace is so easily passed,
A game of hot potato played with strangers—
Peace, the little red ball that makes its rounds,
Quickly swapped before the music stops
As if peace were a plague to be avoided.

Rather peace is passed through unwitting
Acts of kindness, subtle and simple smiles,
Packed in our ordinary exchanges,
Wrapped in seemingly meaningless gestures:
A gift no one knows they need until it's gone.

IONA

Written for the Feast of St. Columba, 2021

I long for the isle of Iona,
To leave these muddy shores and set forth for
The Hebrides. Maybe there I'll find rest
And lose myself in the books that once lined
Her phantom halls, each carefully illumed with
Invisible ink. And there I'll learn to pray,
Miming the movements of grey saints long gone,
Mouthing along to their ancient songs:
Psalms and more psalms. Over and over again
Till the repetition fades and every
Word sounds the same, all drawl and drawn.
But the shore is long and the tide is rough
And men like me aren't made for sea.
I know I'll never see Iona.
St. Columba, would you pray for me?

THE HOURS

Written at Holy Cross Monastery, West Park, NY.

I. Arrival

The car wound its way down the winding road,
The tall pines on either side walling us in,
Signaling to the driver and I,
Leave the noise of the world behind.
The silence set in and I was alone.
The driver now a distant sight from the
Valley below. The silence pressed in and
As I sat in my room, I wondered if
I could survive deprived of noise, or be driven
Mad by the echoes in those hollow halls.
The Great Silence began and I
Was adrift, with neither distraction
    Nor interruption to tether me fast,
    Drifting, into the void—God's grand expanse.

II. Matins

The bell tolled as the sun rose and I
Fought myself to get up from my bed,
Wrestling with those warm sheets begging me
To ignore the bells and risk a little sleep.
And as I stumbled into morning prayer
I fought to stay awake, doing my best
To stifle my yawns and follow along.
I was losing that battle, but to my
Surprise I wasn't alone.
A monk, about ninety, lifted his hand
To cover his mouth while his brothers sang.
He gave me a knowing look, a smile,

And while Jacob wrestled with God
We did out best to subdue the beast of sleep.

III. Holy Eucharist

The bread snapped with a sharp crack sending shivers
Down the length of my spine, reminding me
Of my frailty and the life I'll one day
Leave behind. We're as frail as broken bread.
It's no wonder the symbol works so well,
The host in the abbot's hand, straining, waiting—
A hanged man dangling from the gallows,
A carpenter hanging from a cross.
And me, suspended between prayers,
Waiting to break, burst, split into two,
Hanging from a hope I no longer hold,
    A host in the hand of an angry God.
    The gifts of God for the people of God.

IV. Diurnum

The sun rides high on the valley's slope,
Cresting the tree line, darting in and out
Of cloud cover like a child hiding his
Face, amused by his sudden disappearance.
But that game gets old fast and I'm no longer
Amused. It's too cold to play hide and seek
And we both have jobs to do. But the sun
Neither hears nor cares and I'm too small to
Demand its attention. And if that's true
Of the sun, I can only imagine
God—too big to hear or care, or so I'm told
By those who've tried to get his attention—
    Lobbing pebbles at his marble windows.
    (The fruitless click-clack they call prayer.)

V. Vespers

There was a bend in his back from bending
To pray. His head perpetually floorward,
Stooped from years of faithful service,
Knowing others now from the scuffs on their shoes.
When everyone left the chapel he remained,
Taking longer than most to get up from
His seat, bowing once more to the crucifix
Fixed to the wall at the end of the hall.
Some say he died bent over his bread.
Others say he went knelt by the side of his bed.
But on the day he died, he looked to the sky
And saw the face of God etched into the sun,
  The same face he saw in the stains on the
  Floor and in the shoes his lay-brothers wore.

VI. Compline

Today I prayed to the holy mother
Like I would my own, in short casual
Sentences loaded with meaning and
The little jokes only we would know.
And after I lit the candle's wick
I looked up and saw my mother's face carved
In stone, imposed over the Madonna,
An interloper holding the Christ child.
Then, I remembered what it was to
Be held, nestled in the crook of her arm
Without a care in the world, safe and
Secure between my mother's breasts,
  The whole world held in the cleft of her hand,
  Soothing me to sleep while we waited for dawn.

VII. Departure

Just the birds, the river frozen over,
My words suspended in the winter air,
The chimney smoke rising like incense,
The silence heavy with fervent prayer.
Leave me to the trails, the icons hidden
In leaves, the spectres of holy men
Rising to meet me from the shadows
Cast along the forest's ochre floor.
And there's the city looming gray,
Giants made of steel, imposing themselves
On the sky as if to remind us
Of Babel, of hubris, of the serpent's final words.
    Banished to the wilds, exiled from Eden,
    Just beyond the cloister, back in the world.

THE CONVERSION OF ST. IGNATIUS

St. Ignatius returned to the place where
He traded his blade in exchange for a
Limp; the tomb of the knight he should've been.

There he recalled the cannon fire,
The searing heat, the blazing flame
And the sudden paralyzing pain.

He remembered then the medic's tents,
The endless cycles of breaking and binding,
The empty promises of well-meaning men,

You'll be good as new and this won't hurt a bit,
Before they proceed to break his leg
And begin the cycle all over again.

Maybe that's what it takes to make a saint;
Tragic loss, broken limbs, and a lingering
Limp and maybe broken men make for

Lousy sinners; their limbs a constant
Reminder of who they could've been—
Forever limping, broken, holy men.

NOISE POLLUTION

Someone asked me,
How do you pray
In the city?

The noise must be
a distraction.
The noise isn't

The problem,
The noise is
The prayer—

Eight million
Souls looking
For answers.

PLAYING PRETEND

There was an old tree in our backyard
(But looking back now, it was more like a bush),
Gnarled and overgrown, hollow enough to
Fit a five-year-old's imagination.

Beyond the thin wall of prickling pine
Was a space filled with toys and treasure,
A hoard fit for a juvenile dragon:
Shovels, cars, and little green army men.

We would spend hours playing in the shade,
Balancing on branches, hiding
When our parents called us in for dinner;
Unwilling to leave the real world behind.

Because that world we made was real to us.
In that hollow space, we imagined
Ourselves creators—God speaking, light breaking,
The shadows banished beyond our sight.

SAVANNAH

We took a trip down to Savannah
In a cramped economy class cabin.

They told us it would be easy flying
And that snacks would be provided soon.

But I wasn't worried about the flight,
In fact, I was worried about landing:

That abrupt thump you feel when the wheels touch down
And all that momentum is caught in your throat.

It's the sudden stopping that bothers me,
Gravity pressed against your chest,

Wondering if you'll ever stop at all,
Picturing a fiery end on live TV.

But even after landing I still felt
The weight and having landed I wondered

Was it the landing or where we landed?

THE TRAPPIST WAY

Enter your inner room,
Close the door
And let the light shine in
The form of things unknown.
Displace the shadow
And make space for
The grandeur of God
Found in simple sights and smells.
Enter your room,
Close the door
And look within.
There lies heaven,
The longing heart,
The common well of men.

FORESTRY

The splayed branches cast a shadow
Over the brown grass beneath its
Boughs, reminding me that green things
Die in the shade. The growth
Of the oak comes at the cost
Of the grass, stealing the sun from
The once green sea-bed below,
Killing the womb from which it grew—
The common reward of birthing.

BLAME

The serpent licked his lips
Beckoning the earth-brown girl
To join him in the shade.

There they conversed freely.
He listened to her questions,
Lending her a much-needed ear.

The shade seemed safe enough,
The fruit was bursting with juice
And for the first time, Eve forgot

The rules. Feeling secure
She reached out her hand while the
Snake whispered sweetly in her ear,

Saying all the things she
Wished Adam said (his silent
Face hard as clay, consumed with the

Task of naming). God watched
On and dared not interfere
And somehow, after all these years

She still bears the blame.

THEY KNEW THEY WERE NAKED

They were naked and ashamed, or so the
Good book says, recounting the moment when
Their barren frames were in need of clothes.

An invisible wall between them,
Knit with fig leaves and threaded with mistrust—
The clothing we carefully wear

To guard us against another's touch.
Obscuring the sightlines of anyone
Brazen enough to see us, know us,

And name us. Hiding from inquiring eyes,
Wearing isolation like armor,
An eternity between us:

A chasm we desperately long to bridge,
An impassable pass inches from our skin,
Running short of plank & stone,

Tearing down bridges to wall ourselves in.

DRAINS

The water circled the drain,
Swishing and swirling seven times
Round before settling in the depths
Of Dante's hell, a network of
Pipework filled with silt and soil,
The refuse we conveniently
Wash away, wishing that our sins
would do the same—circle round the
Drain till all that's left is
Bare skin and innocence.

THE SOMME

I remember reading 'bout the trenches,
Flipping through black and white photos of

Mudwalls made with decaying bodies,
Bones picked clean by mortar shell and vermin,
The blank stares of young men grown old too fast,
And the miles of hopeless track cut through the earth.

We were civilized then, or so we said,
And one hundred years later we believe
We're still headed for utopian peace.

We're civilized now, or so we say,
Building Babel on mudwalls and flesh.

I KEEP FORGETTING TO GET THESE DEVELOPED

Dusty canisters of camera rolls
(memories we want to remember
Or nightmares we'd rather forget)

Hidden away in black plastic tubes,
Waiting for the right chemistry to set
Them free. But as long as they stay locked up

We don't have to deal with what they might reveal
(memories we want to remember
Or nightmares we'd rather forget).

LEAVING KABUL

They were packed in like sardine cans.
Anonymous bodies clinging to
Eachother, their worst dream come true:
Leaving a land they loved behind
(drowned now in rivers red as wine)
Desperately gripping a stranger's hand.

ST. JULIAN

And then there's St. Julian,
Locked in her room with her
Calico cat, praying,

Whispering words in her cell
For the world beyond her walls.
Whenever people stopped by

They would ask, *Are you lonely?*
Julian never replied.
She didn't know. All she knew

Was that presence often feels
Like absence and solitude
Like a community of love.

ON SIMON THE SORCERER

Men like Simon always want to know
the price of power, willing to pay
Any toll unless it comes at real cost.

Simon thought Peter would take the silver,
Maybe he heard about Judas' price.
But he couldn't fathom what it truly cost—

The complete and utter denial of self.

ON ST. FRANCIS PREACHING TO THE BIRDS

Written for the Feast of St. Francis, 2021

And so, St. Francis gathered the swallows.
The dapple breasted, the white-winged, the brown,
The elder ones who had forgotten their song,
And the hatchlings who hadn't yet learned to sing.
In a clearing on the far side of town
St. Francis preached to those little birds.
He was motivated by love; a love for
The neglected and the overlooked,
The little creatures we often ignore,
Avian neighbors we never consider.

And if Francis can find beauty in them
Maybe our neighbors are beautiful too;
Overlooked and ignored in our passing by,
Rejected for the dappled spots they wear.
And if we can learn to preach to birds,
Loving our neighbors might come easy.
It's in the winged things we see the Father's
Care, his compassion for the rejected,
The seeming insignificant,
The men and women we often ignore.

FUNERARIA LA FE

We could hear their wails through the walls,
The weeping and groaning of loss,
And every so often we listened
And heard a vague impression of
A eulogy. We lived above
A funeral home, just above
Where they rolled the caskets in
And sometimes we stared outside
To watch the shapes in black garbs
Welcome their loved ones home.

FISHING

My father took me fishing
At a lake upstate.
I was about ten,
Too young to wait by
A lakeside and too young
To appreciate the art,
The world-weary patience
Required to sit and do
Nothing. Peace was boring,
Like all young boys
I wanted action.
But my father didn't listen,
He simply motioned
With his finger
For me to sit still.
And all these years later
I still see his finger
Pressed against his lips,
Inviting me to be still
Lest I miss the moment.

ON PICKING UP MY FATHER'S FOUNTAIN PEN

The ink pools beneath the nib
Like a black lagoon
Or some Scottish lock,
Deep and dark,
Spreading like a blood splatter
Across the virgin page;
Evidence of consummation,
The deed done.
The task of creation
Like procreation—
Best done at night
Under full view of the moon,
My lunar voyeur
Watching me like a hawk
Circling its prey,
Biding its time
Before it strikes.
Talons taught
And ready,
Itching to feel flesh and blood,
Dirt and mud.
To catch and release,
Murder and steal.
The poet watching,
Observant and objective.
Writing as if under a spell,
Aware and unaware.
Sinking in a pool of ink.
Desperately gasping for air.

CHARLIE

We brought Charlie home in a great glass case
And placed him carefully on my bureau.

He was small back then. Red streaks ran down his
Side like great bursts of brilliant flame,

Paddling about in the water
Like a fiery comment cutting through space.

I spent hours with my nose pressed against his
Tank, watching him hunt for bobbing pellets

In the water. As far as I could tell
He was my first friend, my first confidant,

The last emblem of my innocence.
But like innocence, pet-store turtles

Don't last very long and after Charlie died
It was safe to say my boyhood was gone.

TRAINSPOTTING

A train hurtles past my window
And I barely notice the sound.

Its bumps and beeps are disregarded,
Drowned out by grown indifference.

A train!, my niece exclaims.
Look padrino, a train!

I see it, come, let's watch the train.
Side by side we sit and wait

And all the while I wonder
Why do I ignore the trains?

ON MISSING OUR CONNECTING FLIGHT

We missed our connecting flight,
Stranded in a podunk town,
Stuck between where we were
And where we needed to be.

These disconnections happen often,
Small derailments that interrupt
And throw us off balance,
Forcing us to examine

The roads we've taken
And the paths we've trod.
Forcing us to stop
And consider our course.

Because a podunk town
May have more to offer than we
Realize and maybe
An interruption was

Exactly what we needed.

THIS COFFEE WAS MADE WITH LOVE

My wife tells me
The coffee she makes
She makes with love.

We use the same pot.
We grind the same beans
And I still prefer hers.

Maybe the secret
Is in the giving:
The rejection of

Self-reliance and
The acceptance of
something freely given,

To know she expects
Nothing in return,
Save for gratitude.

BREAKFAST

The bacon sizzles and pops,
Providing percussion for

The bubbling baritone
Of the coffee pot.

The sound of breakfast is
Almost as good as the smell—

An unexpected chorus
To welcome the sun.

ON WRITING

Its all
X's and O's,
Scribbled lines,
Scratch marks,
And chicken scratch.
Failed rhymes,
Broken metres,
And elusive words.
At least that's how it starts.
Then suddenly
It all comes together.
Our divergent trails
Form a road
To get us where
We're trying to go.

ON SPEAKING

Speaking is more than
Communication, in
Sounding syllables
We give intellection
To meaningless sound,
Crafting consonants
With croaks and groans,
Imbuing scattered
Sound with meaning.
And from this jumbled mess
Emerges the impossible;
The formless formed,
Airy nothingness given shape.
The first creative act
Born again in mortal speech.

CAMP COMANCHE

They dropped us off,
Two adolescent
Campers in the woods,
Barely old enough
To know to miss home
Or the difference
Between a weekend
And a lifetime.

CAMP LESSONS

We were playing hide and seek at midnight
In a grove of grey firs outside of camp,
The quiet night filled with the sound of
Rustling leaves and young men snickering.
I found a hiding spot in a hollowed-
Out tree trunk and turned off my flashlight.
That's when it set in, the overwhelming
Feeling of being alone, deserted,
Unsure if I'd ever be found, unable
To see five feet in front of me, longing
To turn my flashlight on and give myself
Away. With one quick click of a button
I could dispel the shadows that clung to me
And beat back the encroaching darkness,
But something in me decided to resist.
Maybe, it was because I wanted to win
Or maybe, at twelve, I'd realized the truth;
That every life is filled with shadows
And rather than fight them, it's best to learn
To embrace them and make them our own.

DISSIDENTS

There is a sense in which we are
All dissidents, rebels-
Protesting the inevitable,
Fighters straining against time,
Desperately trying to stall the hand
That ticks ever on despite us.
Yet we still protest, demanding
That our years extend beyond
The time we've been allotted,
As if to say, we deserve more
And eighty some-odd years aren't
Enough. It is never enough.
In the end, we'll take an extra
Minute, we'll settle for a breath,
Protesting the inevitable,
Dissidents to the end.

RAM'S HILL ROAD

Up the hill and on the left of Ram's hill road
Stood an old chapel boarded up and shut.
The bells were silent, robbed of their song
But the garden was green and the grasses were cut.

The tulips bloomed bright, all tended with care,
The hedges were neat, all trimmed into rows,
The boughs were heavy with juice laden fruit,
While the church lay dead the garden had grown.

Then I saw him, a priest, withered thin and grey,
His robes brown with soot, his nails black with dirt,
His face beet red from too long in the sun,
His cassock frayed where he kneeled in the earth.

This was his cathedral, the trees were his flock,
His mass was the tilling, his church the soil,
His sermon was silence, his hymns the dew,
The holy, present in his mundane toil.

He handed me a spade, *come and pray with me,*
Join me in the worship of all good things,
The dappled chorus of Nature's sons,
The hymn all green things sing when they sprout for spring.

AN UPTURNED CAN

Spilled paint seeps from an upturned can.
A homicide of color
On the side of the road.

The indigo ink sinks
Into every crack and crevice
Creating little running rivers

In the grey canvas below.
And one has to wonder,
Where did the artist go

And how unattended paint
Contains a beauty all its own?
Flowing freely, painting,

Coating the concrete
Like Pollock, a mural fit for
A gallery, abandoned

On the side of the road.

WOUNDS

In my deepest wound, I saw Your Glory, and it dazzled me.
—SAINT AUGUSTINE

Wounds are ugly things,
They fester and reek
And stink of death.

Even when they heal
They are painful
Reminders of who

We used to be.
But somewhere beneath
Our bloody flesh

Your glory resides.
You dwell in our wounds
And make them your home.

You consecrate
The desecrated
And call our wounds your own.

LA ISLA

I.

The Morning is filled with the sound of
Island birds singing and angry engines,
A chorus accompanied by the soft
Percussion of rain playing on the tin roof.

But as the engines fade into the distance
The birds carry their songs to a new perch,
Leaving behind a familiar silence
Accompanied by the soft percussion of rain.

II.

We awoke to the sound of church bells;
Great pious gongs beckoning the masses,
Dispelling the last remnants of darkness,
Bridging the gap between heaven and hell.

It's Sunday and we are still half asleep,
Enjoying the sound of the morning bells
From our sanctuary—between our bed sheets.

III.

Mama Clara offered us her hands—
Brown withered things full of life and grace,
Calloused from where she clasped her hands to pray.

She took our hands, held them in a vice grip,
Rooting us in place while prayer flowed
From her lips: secret words shared in tongues unknown.
The amen came quick, her hands loosened

And our hands, which were barely holding on,
Started to feel strong once again.

IV.

Peace and quiet are passing things,
Brief and beautiful distractions.
Here today, gone tomorrow,
Like clouds passing under the moon.

V.

I thought I'd do some writing here
And treat the ocean like my muse
But like the ocean, the blank page
Is a terrible mistress.
All at once, she is calm seas and
Storm clouds. Predictably chaotic
And unwilling to be tamed.
But every once in a while
She calms enough to open up
And blesses us with treasures from the deep.

VI.

The sea laps somewhere off in the distance,
Playing a game of tag with the shore.
Always coming and going, never staying,
Forever keeping one foot out the door.

But even waves need to find their rest;
A still tide where they can lay their head
Before once again, pulled by the moon,
They are forced to leave their coral beds.

PHOTOGRAPHS

If only life were as simple as a
Photograph. Black & white with little room
For grey. I wish it were that simple.
In a photo, you can pick out the shadows
And with the turn of a knob make dark things bright.
But life is all color and chaos
And shadows often intermingle with
Light. The neat little boxes we make
Never seem to work. They often bruise
And wound, oversimplifying the complex,
Reducing our neighbors to abstractions—
Black and white photos we happily pick apart.

DISTANCE

Distance: the space between what is and what could be,
The impassable gap of silence
We let hang in the air between us—
Forever suspended in animation,
Faces frozen with penchant words
(all the things we want to say
And all the things we've left unsaid)
Waiting for the other to make a move,
Eyes fixed on each other's lips
As we wait for the other to break the silence.
And we both know we need to speak
But the fear of fallout prevents us
From saying what needs to be said,
Each of us waiting for the right moment,
Knowing that moment will never come.

LITTLE FLOWERS FROM SAINT FRANCIS

I.

Great grace isn't needed
For lengthy prayers and
Late night vigils,
That's the easy stuff.

Grace is needed when
The ego rears
Its ugly head,
Casting stones at
Innocent souls,

Demanding vengeance
Instead of repentance.

Great grace is needed
To overcome the self.
To suffer in silence
The violence of men.

II.

It's easier to hear
God's condemnation
Rather than his grace

And so we fill his mouth
With words he never said,
Hoping to pay penance.

But when he goes to speak
He tends to go off script,
Pronouncing pardon

Instead of wrath;
Subverting the words
We put in his mouth.

III.

Sometimes following God
Looks like spinning round in place,
Unsure where to go, a holy
Disorientation.

But it's only then, when we've lost
All sense of direction,
That we find the path
That we were looking for.

IV.

There's treasure to be found on the breadline,
In those souls for whom no one seems to care
(Ignored by those who worship plenty's shrine).

Blessed are those who don't avert their stares,
Who see the holy in those on the breadline,
And attend to angels unaware.

V.

God usually uses
The unlikely to speak,
Gracing the lips of
Fools and asses alike.

VI.

It's better to savor
Prayer than it is to
Savor food. We need prayer
More, not because we don't need
To eat, but because
Food never satisfies
What our souls require.

VII.

Rewarded are those who rise in the night
To pray—there they will find Christ patiently
Waiting to receive those willing souls,
Those who know that God is often found in
The dead of night—the places light cant reach.

VIII.

It's the bursting and breaking,
The trampling and crushing
That turns grapes into fine wine.
The violence they suffer
Fills the chalices of men,
The breaking they endure
Fills the wedding guests with mirth.
And so like grapes our breaking
Produces perseverance
And it's in our crushing
The evil one is crushed.

IX.

Driven by hunger men go mad,
Willing to lose their souls to fill

Their bellies--betraying the image
God gave them to wear. Consumed by
Scarcity, they seek to devour
Their fellow-men, unable
To curb their all-consuming
Appetites. But what if we fed
The wolves, called them brother, and met
Their needs. Wouldn't then the violence
Cease—when we all have enough to eat,
Sharing in the gifts of God,
Quieting the wolf within,
Realizing that generous
Hearts make for a world of plenty.

X.

In a garden overgrown with weeds
The only solution is to pluck them
Into oblivion—knees in the dirt
Digging out every last rebellious root.

The same can be said of sin, the only
Solution is to dig up our desires
And lay them bare in the sun—allowing
The sun to dry out the sin in our souls.

SHEPHERDING

I sit down to write like
A shepherd herding sheep,
Chasing down wayward words
Like rebellious rams
Refusing to be penned.

FLYING OVER THE ADIRONDACKS

From here the mountains look like molehills,
Great peaks reduced to low rising mounds,
And for a moment we forget their height
And how small we feel in their shadow.

NATIVITAS

No one really talks about the pain,
Her labored breathing filling the stable,
Sweat and blood making mud out of dirt.
The pain is so intense she forgets her name
And knowing that tonight could be fatal
All she thinks about is surviving the birth.
But this is the cost of redemption,
Searing pain surging through a woman's navel
As she's covered in animal refuse and earth—
The all too human work of descension,
The timeless bound up in her belly's girth.

ET VERBUM CARO FACTUM EST

The word became flesh
And no one noticed
Save for a few
shepherd boys minding
Their business, outcasts
At the edge of the world,
The only ones
to witness that great
Miracle: God enfleshed,
The best-kept secret
In all creation,
The harrowing of hell
In human form;
Hidden from the eyes
Of those deemed deserving.
Revealed to those
Humble enough to see.

THE PRESENTATION

Imagine Saint Simeon holding the babe—
Wrapped in rags, toes curled, legs bent
In a fetal state, sleeping, unbothered,
Unaware of old Simeon's tears
Or the weight of the cross that awaits.
And as Simeon weeps Mary watches on,
Pride and dread welling up in her breast,
Her child, once light in the cleft of her arms
Now heavy with the weight of Israel's wait.

179TH STREET

They would emerge from the earth
Like naked mole rats
Who had never seen the sun.

Each step seemed labored
As they climbed the steps
Up and out of the station.

They came from all walks of life,
A gallery's worth
Of human potential

Bearing the marks of their station
In the wrinkled lines
Across their faces.

Heads bent low, they dispersed
In all directions,
Covering the cardinal points,

Moving in robotic rhythm,
Following the migratory
Paths calling them home.

And there we would name them,
Giving the faceless faces
In an attempt to see our own.

SACRIFICE

Our tent was filled with water.
The rain had snuck in while we slept
And left about an inch
Of precipitation behind.

We had forgotten the tarp,
A fatal mistake,
And if not fatal,
At least unbearable.

I remember shivering
In the dark, teeth rattling
In my head like maracas,
My whole body possessed by
Involuntary shaking,

Covered head to toe
In goosepimpled flesh.
Too cold to speak and
Too old to ask for help.

But my father took me in his arms
And laid me on his chest,
Covering me with a dry quilt
While he lay in a pool of water.

The next morning my
Father woke with a cold
And as I watched him sniffling and snorting
I wondered if I'd do the same—

Lay myself down like an island
And freeze on another's behalf.

WIND CHILL

Its thirty degrees and the wind feels
Like its peeling away my skin,
Exposing my bare musculature
To the cruel sting of the elements
Until all that remains is bare bone;
The innards we hide from winter's watchful eye.

But the cold sees past all our pretense,
The clever lies we tell ourselves
To justify, to hide, all those things
We lock up inside—the truth that sets men free,
The real self we cover up in layers
Hoping to hide the scars on our skin.

But winter is no respecter of persons.
We can try to bundle up all we like,
Wrap ourselves in jackets and scarves
In hopes that the chill won't make its way in.
But we know too well, the winter wind
Will win the day, exposing the false self

We love to wrap our lives in.

ON BLOOMING

Flower buds tend to bloom in secret.
Waiting for no one, they pull their petals apart
To display their hidden works of art
To empty green fields, captivating
The sky and all who might pass by with
Their unassuming beauty. Flowers don't feel shame,
They feel no qualms about their naked frame,
They revel in the exposure, longing
To be looked upon, enjoyed, observed,
Knowing that their beauty is fleeting.
When their petals bloom, then begins the bleeding,
Till all that's left is a withered memory—
The natural course of aging things,
The price they pay for the joy they bring.

MEISTER ECKHART

It is in darkness one finds the light, in sorrow,
this light is nearest to us.
—MEISTER ECKHART

In the darkness, Meister Eckhart found light,
He dove deep into the sorrow and found
In that fallow ground the presence of God.

Like a miner searching for hidden gems,
We too seek the luminous in the shadows,
The glory veiled in shrouds of velvet night;

For its in absence that we find presence
And it's in the eye of the storm that we
discover the comfort we've been looking for.

ISAIAH'S VISION

In every age violence seems to reign,
Exerting its will on a weary world
With its iron fist clenched and curled,
Ready to strike those who defame its name.
We spend too much time justifying it's
Presence—savoring the peace it brings,
Ignoring how it turns men to things,
And casualties we too casually omit.
Maybe, our swords make for better plowshares.
Instruments of death transformed into
Instruments of life—a new lens to see through,
Exposing us to the other's cares,
Breaking the cycle of life for life,
Dispelling the lie that might is right.

COGNITIVE DISSONANCE

It takes cognitive dissonance to hate
Someone else made in the image of God.

For in them we catch a glimpse of ourselves
And through them, we ascertain the divine.

SPEECH ACT THEORY

What if we learned to read slowly?
Savoring each sound over and over
Again till all the marrow is drained
And there is nothing left to savor.

What if we took the psalmist seriously
And spent our days and nights thinking over
Every last word that has ever been said,
Refusing to leave a single noun behind?

What if we learned to see beneath our words?
The hidden worlds wedged between the lines,
The small impressions left behind by
The author waiting to be revealed.

Maybe, if we learned to read slowly
Our speech would be measured--carefully used,
Well thought out, free from the cycle of urgency
That causes us to speak before we think.

And if we took the time to measure our words
We would learn to see THE WORD behind
Our words, the one we seek in all human speech,
The utterance who uttered us into being.

THE SUM OF THINGS

It's never just one cup of coffee,
In fact, it's every cup of coffee
I've ever had distilled into a
Single sip with the same compounding force
Of a neutron star collapsing into bits.

And it's never just one hello, in fact,
It's every hello I've ever shared
Summed up in one eternal greeting,
Every human moment of meeting
Bound up in a single five-letter word.

Every moment is just that, a myriad
Of moments and memories interweaved
Into a single time in space, reflecting
All that came before and all that could be;
Eternity frozen in place, drawing

Our eyes beyond the moment
And into time's intricate web,
Begging us to see beyond ourselves,
(the fleeting vapor we call life)
And to see our place in the storm.

VICTORINOX

My father handed me
A red Swiss Army Knife.
One by one he showed me
The tools–the blade and saw,
The philips and flathead,
All coated in
Stainless steel chrome.

It was heavy then
And I held it with care
Like a wounded dog,
Ready for the bite.
But then he said,
Cut away from yourself,
Watch your fingers when you close.

This isn't a toy,
This isn't meant for boys.
This is a tool,
A man's tool, dangerous
And useful. Keep it sharp,
Keep it clean, keep it close.
This isn't meant for boys.

I began by gingerly
Whittling wood, running the blade
Along the skin of aspen twigs,
Cutting my name into
Decaying bark,
Growing more confident
With each pass of the penknife,

Repeating my father's words
In my head like a
Mantra, *this isn't a toy,*
This isn't meant for boys.
This is a tool,
A man's tool, dangerous
And useful.

It's smaller now,
Resting in my palm,
More bark than bite,
Wielded with a deft hand,
And a confident stroke.
Cut away from yourself,
I say, *This isn't a toy.*

This isn't meant for boys.
This is a tool, a man's tool—
Dangerous and useful.
Keep it clean.
Keep it close.
Keep it sharp.
Edges dont care for age.

SILENCE AND SOUND

You dont know silence until its silent—
The great booming void,
A cacophony of empty space
Enveloping your senses
In waves of nothing.
But between the streetcars
And rumbling trains
Silence is always silent.
All there is is noise
And the foreboding feeling
That noise is all there is.

CARTOGRAPHY

As a young boy, I was obsessed with maps.
I would spend hours tracing the black lines that
I eventually learned were borders.
In my mind's eye, I plotted journeys
To distant lands where the soil was pink and blue
And the seas were cut into patterned grids.
I would imagine climbing over the
Slate black lines that separated nations,
Tunneling under the walls dividing
Sovereign lands, wondering who the builders
Were and what possessed them to erect
Black gates between neighbors and friends.

***

We took a road trip down I-95,
Crossing state line after state line
And while we drove I searched in vain
For the seams I saw sketched on my father's map.
My father told me that boundaries were
Imagined—political lies invented
To divide districts and divvy up wealth.

Five year old me found the whole concept
Absurd and thirty year old me finds
the whole project disturbing.

FLOORBOARDS

The floor squeaks under my pressured step,
Moaning in relief as I release my weight,
Only to groan as my foot falls again.

I try to walk softly, lifting my heels,
Releasing each toe one at a time,
Trying my best to silence my steps,

To walk lightly, as they say. Tip-toeing
Across the grain of the floor, cognizant
Of those spaces I often ignore.

But it doesn't matter what I do
Or how lightly I take my steps,
The floor is always howling, aching

Under the weight, screeching and squealing
With every measured step. Wailing beneath the
Pressure—the curse of its existence—

The torture that comes with holding.
The cursed burden we call bearing.

TRANSUMANAR

We were dancing along a sunbeam—
My best friend and I skipping between shadows,
Pretending that light was something to ride,

Crossing the Rosen bridge, braving the Bifrost,
Following Beatrice's virgin gaze
Into Apollo's grand expanse.

And there, in my backyard, we watched the light
Transform the morning dew into
Brilliant bursts of rainbow buds,

Turning branches and leaves into
Stained glass and shadow-work. And when the light
Fell on our skin we felt the sun's gentle tug,

The upward pull of the solar tide,
The great font further out and further in
Dragging us under its gentle stream.

And then, without a care in the world,
We danced. For the first time feeling free,
Our feet no longer fit for dirt,

Passing beyond what was, into what is,
Caught up in the rapture of passion—
All fire, all flame, all beauty, and good.

But, we were just boys staring into the sky
And what we saw passed as quickly as it came.
A fleeting taste of future glory—

The brief brilliance of a setting sun.

LOOK AT THE BIRDS

All we know is toil, living's hard work,
The never-ending grind wearing us down
Until we're nothing but ash and dirt.

We all long for silence's sound.
The peace of stillness, the good work of rest.
The fallow earth broken for softer ground.

Come, lay your head down and quiet your breath.
Learn to cease. Remember 'gain how to be—
The silent months spent at your mother's breast.

Contemplate the birds, look at them flying free,
Trusting the wind to hold them aloft,
The same unhurried breath you need to breathe—

Hands open to receive both peace and loss,
No longer straining or striving,
Open to blessing, burden, and cross.

THE BAY-CROW

A crow out of place above the bay
Cackling at some invisible foe.
A shadow over the foot of the sea,
Blacker than Tartarus, mocking the sun.

Its his kingdom now, perched on the rocks
A triumphant king crowned in feathered night.
A usurper and invader come to pillage
And plunder the sand dunes and blue lagoons.

His beak covered in gull blood and fish scales,
He invites his murder to join the fray
And commands the tide with bloodied caws;
All solitude and haunting symbol.

SUNDAY STEW

The pot was old. Scratched black and worn from use.
She held it in one hand while her other stirred,
Carefully watching her sauce reduce
While the meat rested on her cutting board.
And like the pot, she was old and worn.
Valleys of age cut across her face,
Digging deep furrows in the smile she wore.
The fleeting flow of time etched into place.
Both her and the pot: scratched, black, and old,
Hollow containers filled to the brim,
Bathing in fire to banish the cold,
The unassuming front hiding what's within—

    The nourishment we all desperately need,
    A broth to water our souls-in-seed.

VINIFICATION

Words are like heavy grapes on a vineyard vine.
You must find the right ones, gather them together,
And wring out whatever meaning you can.
Then, let them sit. After a year or two,
Come back, and you will have found something worth saying.

THE END IS NIGH

The end is nigh read the sign,
Apocalyptic doom scrawled
Across a scrap of cardboard.
But the seminarian
Paid it no mind. Assured of
His eternal reward he
Crossed the street without thinking
And walked right into the path
Of an oncoming hearse.
The end is nigh read the sign.
And in his last moments,
Before his last rites, he resolved
To become the patron saint
Of warnings—cardboard signs and
Traffic lights alike.

AN UNHOLY OBSERVATION

I sat in the corner of the room,
Near enough his bedside to see his face,
But far enough away ii make my anger known.

They'd rushed in like cattle in a frenzy,
Posturing and pushing past one another
Like they were fighting for courtside seats.

But thats just how church folks are, turning
Every social gathering into
A twisted contest for the pious,

Peacocks preening their feathers before the Lord
And whoever else may be watching.
God forbid if no one is watching.

You see my grandfather was dying
And the whole church had come out to visit,
To sing songs and attempt a healing.

Though, who would want to come back from THAT?
But abuelo was as pious as they came
And even though they werent there for him,

He was there for them. And from my corner
I watched him hold court, silent and smiling
Singing along with what was left of his voice.

Above his head hung the Christ on the cross,
Gaunt and frail and modestly clothed,
And there was abuelo, his spitting image,

Praying for the sinners sat at his side.
Christ between the thieves praying the same,
Father forgive them they dont know what they do.

HESTIA

We gathered round the hearth,
Hestia's throne,
And let her yellow tongues
Lick our cold bitter bones.

Of course, no one spoke.
There was nothing left to say.
Instead, we sat in silence
And wondered if

Ole Hestia had the power
To dispel
The cold front between us—
That bitter, inhospitable land

Neither of us were willing to cross.

THE HULDUFOLK

Mind the faerie roads. We chuckled, but
Our host in Reykjavik wasn't joking.
He had the look of a man who'd seen
Something he couldn't explain, just behind his
Eyes in the dark corners of his mind.

He was talking of course about the
Huldufolk, what us moderns call Elves
And dismiss as a pagan superstition
From a Pre-Christian past, a legend meant to
Spook the occasional tourist passing through.

But under the stars, in the dead of night,
Miles from the village, and out on the fjord,
I believed in the Huldufolk too.
Who wouldn't? For the wilds remind us,
That for all our progress, they are wilder still.

MIDDLE CLASS

We were the wrong kind of poor,
Too wealthy for the breadline and
Just broke enough to make ends meet.

Somewhere between the haves
And the have nots we eeked out
A living, paying what we could,

Living check to check while
The bills piled up and
Our savings ran dry.

But each month we made it.
The budget balanced out
And our debt was in the black.

But when the country ran out of cash,
I couldn't help but laugh.
Maybe our senate should learn
A thing or two from the

Middle Class.

PENANCE

Wait 'till we're finished praying.
My mom slapped my hand away
From the steaming pile of bread
Set between the rice and beans.
I jerked my hand back, annoyed,
Hungry, and ready to eat.

Prayers in my family
Tended to drag on.
We prayed for everything
But the food. Tonight was no
Different. My dad rambled on
And on and on and on,
Stuck in an endless loop of
Amens and hallelujahs.

But while everyone's eyes were closed
I shot my hand out and snatched
A smoking dinner roll
From under my mother's nose
And just before the amen
I stuffed the roll into my mouth.
All I felt was pain. My tongue
Was burnt to a crisp and
Every tastebud screamed in pain,

And though we weren't Catholic
I was well aware of penance,
The price of impatience
And God's sick sense
Of situational humor.

TULSA

We drove through the backwoods of Tulsa
In a hatchback red with fading rust

Pass red-wood barns, water towers, and
Miles and miles of open field

Where herds of black cattle crowded the golden lawns
Like dust mites circling 'round a sunbeam—

A remnant of a bygone age where men
Knew the land and pasture and prairie

Were one and the same: wild and untamed, endless and
Free, all horizon line and zephyr sky.

There we were, cutting cross country,
Admiring the view like a postcard,

Rumbling down the flat black asphalt
Unaware of the irony,

Enjoying the seeming boundless stretch
While driving along a boundary.

SANTA ANA

Santa Ana.
San Miguel.
San Joaquin.
Street names,
Petitions,
Summoning invocations.
Offering direction
In more ways than one.

ATTRITION

Follow the wind
And let it whip your sails full.

Give into the tide,
The tug and the pull.

Allow the music to take you
And fill you whole.

Give into the rhythm,
The drum and the bass.
Allow the snare to capture your soul.

Give your senses over
To the senseless and wild.
Let the unfamiliar lead you astray
And summon the courage to give into the now.

Forget the hours,
The years,
The winding days.
Savor the short-term.

Let it all slip away.

ROSARY

I made my way round the beads,
Praying in circles.
Unsure where to stop
Or how to end.
An endless loop of silent amens,
Turning in on themselves
Like paper-folds.
A bit like origami—
Wondering when
The mindless moves
Will finally make sense.